FREQUENCIES

Artful Essays
Volume 1 ~ Fall 2012

TWO DOLLAR RADIO
Books too loud to ignore

Copyright © 2012 by Two Dollar Radio
All rights reserved
ISBN: 978-1-937512-01-9

Cover: *Mr. Fix-it*, copyright 2011 by John Gagliano.
All interior illustrations: Copyright 2012 by John Gagliano.
Photographs in 'Seven Interruptions of the Image': Morgan Kendall.

Advertisement images are all in the Public Domain:
Page 7: *Woman Owner in her Grocery Store in Leakey, Texas, with a Friend, near San Antonio, 05/1973*, Photographer: St. Gil, Marc, U.S. National Archives' Local Identifier: 412-DA-12443.
Page 27: *Nucoa Margerine, Kids on Swing*, Nickolas Muray, 1939, George Eastman House Collection, Accession Number: 1971:0048:0020.
Page 49: *American Cyanamid, Man in Subway*, Nickolas Muray, 1939, George Eastman House Collection, Accession Number: 1971:0050:0017.
Page 86: *W.G. Leistikon, 70, and John Ricks, 87, in Front of the Local Drugstore. Stumps in Front of Store Are Reserved for the "Old-Timers," 11/1972*, Photographer: St. Gil, Marc, U.S. National Archives' Local Identifier: 412-DA-3644.

Typeset in Garamond, the best font ever.
Frequencies custom font created by John Gagliano.
Printed in the United States of America.
No portion of this book may be copied or reproduced, with the exception of quotes used in critical essays and reviews, without the written permission of the copyright holder.

FREQUENCIES

ARTFUL ESSAYS
Volume 1 ~ Fall 2012

OPEN SESAME

BY JOSHUA COHEN

A writer stands outside a story yelling, "Open Sesame!" and the story, as if a seed, opens. And treasure is found inside. That treasure, of course, is just another story, and it all begins again…

Or else, say the writer is no different from any other of his tribe—say he's actually a thief. And the story is no story, but really a mountain. "Open Sesame!" (this writer continues)—the mountain opens and my meaning is revealed.

A version of this nonsense—this magician's stage-business—occurs in the tale *Ali Baba and the Forty Thieves*, popularly known from the *1001 Nights*.

But Ali's tale is not to be found in the oldest manuscripts of that collection. Some scholars believe it to be the invention of one Youhenna Diab, known as Hanna of Aleppo, an Arab Christian storyteller said to have communicated it to Antoine Galland, the first translator of the *Nights* into French. Others argue for a purely Western source, and believe that *Ali* is the incorrupt fiction of Galland himself (though Richard Burton, the first translator of an unexpurgated *Nights* into English, claimed that *Ali* was to be found in an Arabic original, a mythical manuscript often forged but never found).

Indeed Galland (1646-1715) is the earliest source for this famous exclamation: "*Sésame*," he has his Baba say, "*ouvre toi!*" while the ponderous Burton (1821-1890) has given us not "sesame" but "Open, O Simsim!"

In the first two decades of the nineteenth-century, the brothers Grimm collected what would seem to be a German variant under the title *Simeliberg*. In their telling a mountain somewhere in the Reich opens to disclose its myriad riches when addressed with the word *Semsi*: "*Berg Semsi, Berg Semsi, thu dich auf.*" The Grimms, who were, we should remember, philologists and compilers of a dictionary, explain this *Semsi*—given in subsequent editions of their work as *Simsi* and *Semeli*—as an archaic German term, or name, for "mountain."

Wilhelm Grimm, the younger of the brothers and the better writer, notes: "This name for a mountain is, according to a document in Pistorius, very ancient in Germany. A mountain in Grabfeld is called Similes and in a Swiss song a Simeliberg is again mentioned. This makes us think of the Swiss word 'Sinel' for 'sinbel,' round."

Was Ali Baba Galland's creation, or only a character adapted from European folklore? Should we think that Galland, that forty-first thief, in an ostensible translation of Arabic into French, gave us, instead, an immemorial German children's story in Oriental guise? Thus far we have an errant Arab original, a French *sésame* from the seventeenth-century, a German *Semsi* collected in the early nineteenth-century, and an English *Simsim* from later that same century. Our understanding is further complicated when we think that Burton, whose English is the latest of the revisions discussed here, has left us with seemingly the

The most valuable coin has always been with us, within us: the word, the call, whether shared, lent, borrowed, or stolen.

most authentic salutation: His *Simsim* is nothing but the Arabic word for sesame, *Sesamum orientale.*

Which came first, *Simsim* or *Semsi*? *Sésame* or a more germinating seed? As our tale's setting is "the Middle East" (a British fantasy), opinions and arguments support every agenda, obliterating synthesis. While *Sesamum orientale* was prized by Babylon for its ability to repel curses, *Simsim* has been alternatively interpreted as a derivation from Arabic's *shems*, meaning "sun," and even as a corruption of the pacific *Salaam* (*Şemsi* is also a Turkish name, originally an honorific, meaning "the illuminated"). Word-wealthy we might be, but still wedged, between cave walls and protective boulder admitting no light. Information-rich but still greedy, as scholars have been greedy for two centuries, for an Arabic source for a German folktale/French art-story that, in our Englished day, has become the quintessential narrative of Arabia.

The mountain opens for the voice, the voice rolls away the sepulchral stone—reveals the truest treasure: emptiness, proverbial silver, metaphor's gold, echo gleaming unisonous. The most valuable coin has always been with us, within us: the word, the call, whether shared, lent, borrowed, or stolen. There is no cavern more mysterious than the mouth, bound by air and bony ignorance.

I first heard Ali Baba's cry not as a reader of Scheherazade's crepuscular, mortal entertainment, but as a pajamafied fanatic of weekend TV. In loony cartoons come Sundays, with even the scrambled Sinbads and Aladdins and genies and Harun al-Rashids addressing the rockface in gumptious New York immigrantese, "Close, seza me!" (after botching the opening act, with hapless "Open Sarsaparillas," and "Open Saddle Soaps").

I write this in the winter of the eighth and, *Insha'Allah*, last year of an American presence in Iraq—birthplace of the *Nights* (and of writing itself). In Iraq, Ali Baba served as US military slang to characterize "the natives," much as Vietnam's Charlie was used to dehumanize the enemy of that previous lost war. In time, however, many Iraqis themselves began using the epithet to describe the GIs who looted Iraqi museum property, businesses, and homes; soldiers who need demonstrate no causality, nor do they need any magic formula to burst down doors—just force. ■

A SHORT HISTORY OF THE McCLANAHAN FAMILY

BY SCOTT McCLANAHAN

here were 13 of them. The children had names that ended in Y sounds. That night I couldn't sleep so I got out grandma's picture books and I learned about my blood and the names that ended in Y sounds. There was Betty and there was Annie and there was Stirley and there was Stanley and there was Leslie and there was Gary and there was Larry and there was Terry.

Ruby said: "I like names that end in Y."

They all grew up in Danese, WV, eating blackberries for breakfast and eating blackberries for lunch and watching the snow come beneath the door in the wintertime. Holy shit it's cold.

There was my Uncle Stanley who I never heard say anything except "sheeeeeeeeeeeeet" and who I saw at the hospital one night talking to this other guy about how the state of West Virginia was making people wear a helmet now if they rode a 4-wheeler. He was all pissed off about it and told the guy: "I mean they're gonna let them bunch of queers get married now, and I can't even ride my 4-wheeler without a helmet on."

I flipped the page of the picture book and there was my Aunt Betty. She came over one day years ago and sat at our table and told us this story about Elgie. She didn't hold back. She told us the story about how he was trying to get his pension from the mines.

But before he got it, he had to fight for a couple of months. He finally got a letter that went…"Dear Mr. McClanahan, we regret to inform you that we're unable to approve you at this time. Please send your response within seven days and we'll schedule another hearing."

Elgie didn't even say anything.

He just took it down to the outhouse and wiped his ass with it. Then he put it back into the envelope, sealed it up, and sent it back. My Aunt Betty was talking like this was an acceptable thing to do. She was telling this story to her 4-, 5-, 6-year-old and 8-year-old nieces and nephews. This was an acceptable story to tell 8-year-old kids.

We were learning.

There was my Uncle Leslie who was tough as hell. How tough was he? That's what I asked Grandma once. She told me too. She told me about how there was this guy called The Toughest Man in Fayette County and he was this ex-con and beat the hell out of any man who ever messed with him. Leslie and The Toughest Man in Fayette County got into it one day about something. And so Leslie kicked the fuck out of The Toughest Man in Fayette County. It was because the Toughest Man in Fayette County always used vulgar language in front of women.

I asked Ruby, "Well how old was Leslie at the time?"

Ruby was quiet and then she said, "Eleven."

There is one thing you'll never know about my Uncle Nathan. You'll never know just how sweet he was. You'll never know how alive he was.

There were cousins too. There was my Cousin Bonnie who had this little boy from this man named Ernie. And Ernie had been in jail and made his living cockfighting. And so I saw them down at Pizza Hut and I looked over at Ernie and he was holding little Paul in his arms and smacking him in the face. SMACK. SMACK. He was smacking him hard. Everybody in the Pizza Hut was horrified because there was little Paul and he wasn't crying about it. He was laughing.

He was laughing because he loved getting slapped in the face.

BUT STOP!

There is one thing you'll never know about my Uncle Nathan. You'll never know just how sweet he was. You'll never know how alive he was.

Then I looked at pictures of my uncles like Uncle G. My Uncle G. was always trying to kill himself, but something always went wrong. One time he was working in a factory up north and living on Lake Erie. He bought a boat and a shotgun and some shells and decided to go out on the boat on a Saturday morning and end his life. He said goodbye to all of his friends and he told his wife it was the end. He had enough guts now. He wanted people to know this time he was truly going to make it happen. So he cleaned the shotgun and went out in his boat. He shined the boat up the day before. He cranked the motor and went out into the middle of the lake. He sat and looked out over the shining water and thought about his life. He knew this was the end. He clicked off the safety, put the barrel in his mouth and pulled the trigger. Nothing happened. He was still alive.

He cracked open the shotgun and he saw it wasn't loaded. When he cleaned it earlier, he took out the shells. He left the shells on the bed. Shit.

He took his boat back home and he knew things were different now. He never tried to take his life again.

There were stories about little boys getting ear infections, and Ruby not having enough money to take them to the doctors. So they just twisted and turned and flipped and flopped in their sick beds crying for days until their eardrums popped *poof* and they eventually went deaf. What did you say?

My dad was working at Kroger when he was 19 years old, and one day in a store meeting, the manager was saying the names of these guys who broke into the store and stole a bunch of shit. He said the name of one of the robbers: "Stanley McClanahan."

Then he asked my dad, not thinking, "Do you know him Mack?"

My dad said: "Yeah, he's my brother."

So the room grew quiet and the manager later apologized to him.

There was my Uncle Grover who suffered from depression and schizophrenia. And instead of taking him to the doctor they brought in a faith healer and had someone hold him down and tried exorcising his demons. This was the way it was done. DEMONS. There was a picture of Elgie's family I found—all eleven of them lined up in a row and so I asked my grandma, "Well who's that and who's this."

She said—"That's so and so and she killed herself."

Then I said, "Well who's this and who's that."

Ruby said, "O that's so and so—she killed herself."

And out of the 11 children, 5 of them committed suicide.

And so I asked, "Well what happened to Elgie's father?"

She said: "O one day he was rocking a baby in his lap and then he put the baby down and went out behind the Johnny house."

Then she whispered so Nathan couldn't hear: "And then he shot himself."

I flipped through the picture book and I saw it all. Some of them stayed and had children and some of them went to other places. Some went north to places like Flint, Michigan, and Cleveland, Ohio, and worked in factories. And some worked for General Motors in Flint, Michigan, and some worked in steel mills in Cleveland, Ohio. And the girls went to Washington, DC, and worked as secretaries. And some stayed and became convicted felons, and one married a school teacher named Audrey Karen and had a baby named Scott. And some married wives from far away with different accents and had children with different accents too. And so they went to far away places like San Francisco, California, and Washington, DC, and Richmond, VA. And New York City, NY. And they never saw one another and they did what everyone does, they started living the same old boring fucking story. It's a story full of death and dying, living and life, tits and ass and balls and dicks and pussy. It's an old, old, old story that always begins—they begat and they begat and they begat.

Now a million crazy babies explode from our smiles and start running all over the world so wild and screaming, Ahhhhhhh-hhhhhhhhhhhhhhhhhhhhhhhhhhhhhhhhhhhhhhhhhhhhhhhhhhhhh-

hhhhhhhhhhhhhhhhhhhhhhhhhhhhhhhhhhhhhhhhhhhhhhhhh-
hhhhhhhhhhhhhhhhhhhhhhhhhhhhhhhhhhhhhhhhhhhhhhhhh-
hhhhhhhhhhhhhhhhhhhhhhhhhhhhhhhhhhhhhhhhhhhhhhhhh-
hhhhhhhhhhhhhhhhhhhhhhhhhhhhhhhhhhhhhhhhhhhhhhhhh-
hhhhhhhhhhhhhhhhhhhhhhhhhhhhhhhhhhhhhhhhhhhhhhhhh-
hhhhhhhhhhhhhhhhhhhhhhhhhhhhhhhhhhhhhhhhhhhhhhhhh-
hhhhhhhhhhhhhhhhhhhhhhhhhhhhhhhhhhhhhhhhhhhhhhhhh-
hhhhhhhhhhhhhhhhhhhhhhhhhhhhhhhhhhhhhhhhhhhhhhhhh-
hhhhhhhhhhhhhhhhhhhhhhhhhhhhhhhhhhhhhhhhhhhhhhhhh-
hhhhhhhhhhhhhhhhhhhhhhhhhhhhhhhhhhhhhhhhhhhhhhhhh-
hhhhhhhhhhhhhhhhhhhhhhhhhhhhhhhhhhhhhhhhhhhhhhhhh-
hhhhhhhhhhhhhhhhhhhhhhhhhhhhhhhhhhhhhhhhhhhhhhhhh-
hhhhhhhhhhhhhhhhhhhhhhhhhhhhhhhhhhhhhhhhhhhhhhhhh-
hhhhhhhhhhhhhhhhhhhhhhhhhhhhhhhhhhhhhhhhhhhhhhhhh-
hhhhhhhhhhhhhhhhhhhhhhhhhhhhhhhhhhhhhhhhhhhhhhhhh-
hhhhhhhhhhhhhhhhhhhhhhhhhhhhhhhhhhhhhhhhhhhhhhhhh-
hhhhhhhhhhhhhhhhhhhhhhhhhhhhhhhhhhhhhhhhhhhhhhhhh-
hhhhhhhhhhhhhhhhhhhhhhhhhhhhhhhhhhhhhhhhhhhhhhhhh-
hhhhhhhhhhhhhhhhhhhhhhhhhhhhhhhhhhhhhhhhhhhhhhhhh-
hhhhhhhhhhhhhhhhhhhhhhhhhhhhhhhhhhhhhhhhhhhhhhhhh-
hhhhhhhhhhhhhhhhhhhhhhhhhhhhhhhhhhhhhhhhhhhhhhhhh-
hhhhhhhhhhhhhhhhhhhhhhhhhhhhhhhhhhhhhhhhhhhhhhhhh-
hhhhhh

SHIT! ■

ANNE CARSON

BY EMILY PULLEN

Q *To take and modify some terms from gender theory, I've often considered your work to be an exercise in genre-fuck (as opposed to genre-drag). Rather than passing as something else, your pieces shatter our conception of a concretely defined category system. Does the form emerge whole like Athena from the forehead of Zeus? Does it morph and shift? Is it an intentional challenge to yourself as a writer? Could you talk a little about how your unique experiments in form come about?*

experiments in form come about little by little and in the dark
a matter of keeping oneself off balance

Q *With genre-fuck or a project like* NOX, *readers/critics sometimes don't know what to do with it. I'm thinking specifically about commentary from* The Morning News's Tournament of Books. *The judges kept saying "It's... good. But how do I compare it to these other books?" But knowing what to do with it isn't the point. In fact, not knowing what to do with is the point, perhaps. In the throws of loss and grief, we often "don't know what to do with it." Do you try to make your reader uncomfortable? Do you express thought and emotion how you see them, comfort and category be damned?*

comfort or the lack of it is not the point, thinking is the point
to cause people to think is not easy
to cause myself to think is not easy
lack of ease generates a certain kind of alertness that is more
alive to me

Q *You mentioned in the Lannan interview (in 2001) that you occasionally make collage-style books –* Short Talks *and the "Fall of Rome" essay both started this way.* NOX *is so utterly personal in its content. Was there a moment, when you were making it, that you thought or knew it might become a published book? Is* NOX *the first one that was published in close to its true/original form?*

yes NOX is the first that attempts a replica

Q *The pages of* NOX *have this amazing quality – the items on each page appear to be both on the surface of the page and indented into the page. Have you worked with printmaking or letterpress? Is the original book like that? What was it like making this book into something reproducible?*

the original book is a three-dimensional object
my collaborator (Currie) figured out how to make it seem three dimensional even when mass produced, long story short, by means of bad xeroxing
he said we had to "keep the decay" in it

Q *Was the* NOX *project exclusive or were you working on other things at the same time? How long after you wrote* NOX *was it actually published? Seems like it would have been all-encompassing...*

I made NOX in 2001; it was published in 2010
to make it took about 6 months
I was teaching at the time (ancient Greek) and working on the
Sappho book

Q *I've been reading some of the journals my mom left when she died, and its been stirring up lots of memories, mostly simple, quotidian, and not of her, but that I thought I'd forgotten. When your brother reentered your life, were there things that came back, from that earlier time?*

[   ]
[   ]
[   ]

Q *Was gathering ephemera of your brother something you always did, or did it only begin as you began coping with the loss of him?*

I did not (and do not) collect ephemera of anyone, it collects itself

Q *I think the dictionary definitions on the left-hand page might be my favorite part of NOX. You take something that people presume to be somewhat objective and use it to expose the complex and subjective nature of the translation process. Then you inject yourself and your story and your emotions into those definitions through the phrases you create to illustrate meanings. You subvert its presumed objectivity. I remember when it first dawned on me that you were there on those left-hand pages — you were showing "the truth by allowing it to be seen hiding." Is creating definitions like that ever part of your regular translation process, or is it unique to NOX?*

I have always tried to inject a "created definition" or two into academic work

Q *So much of* Eros the Bittersweet *is about Lack and Longing as they relate to Desire. Not defining something but rather creating an outline around it with words to show us its shape. I'm reminded of Faulkner's Addie Bundren, the focal point of* As I Lay Dying *who is granted her own voice only once. She says: "I would think about his name until after a while I could see the word as a shape, a vessel, and I would watch him liquefy and flow into it like cold molasses flowing out of the darkness into the vessel, until the jar stood full and motionless: a significant shape profoundly without life like an empty door frame; and then I would find that I had forgotten the name of the jar." Did you formerly, or do any of your projects now make as their goal filling in that shape, rather than creating the outline? Or is the outline the goal of translation since the words rarely exactly match?*

[   ]
[   ]
[   ]
[   ]

Q *I remember being pleasantly surprised to hear reference to your books during the first episode of the Showtime series* The L Word. *Then I imagined lots of (possibly superficial, probably not intellectual) lesbians flocking to your work, expecting some sort of romantic, lesbian Neruda-esque lyrical poetry and finding something so utterly different. Did you get any interesting feedback from that cameo?*

my students at that time told me to watch the show, I forgot to

Q *Do you ever think about "the reader" as you're translating or writing? Or is it mostly between you and the text, and then you share the result with the reader later?*

I always think about the reader
the reader's stillness
into which something comes ∎

SEVEN INTERRUPTIONS OF THE IMAGE

WORDS BY BLAKE BUTLER

PHOTOGRAPHS BY MORGAN KENDALL

WILD RUINS

WARDROBE

Untitled Photo

My Parent's House

YELLOW DRESS

ALL MY BAGS ARE PACKED

BLOSSOMS

WILD RUINS

My sister emails me the link to the website with the catalog of photographs she has taken in her recent days of life. As I open the webpage a siren outside the house that we grew up in moves into ear range where I sit at this machine. The light against the white under-mesh of the curtains in this room is too bright in this hour of the sun's rising to let me see the street. Is someone dead. Within one mile of this house my father is in a building full of people he does not know. This is where he sleeps now. At night my mother still sleeps in the bed they've shared for the majority of my life. The bed before that bed is at my sister's house now, I believe, where she sleeps beside her husband. Perhaps it is a different bed. Perhaps I am mixing up beds that have come from this house where now on this machine I click again to see the picture my sister calls *Wild Ruins*. In the foreground a brown horse with a white spot on his forehead leans in such a way to make a tripod of his sternum against the ground as he leans to eat the grass. The grass will go into him to be burned in his cells and give him life. Not far behind the front horse in the image two other horses stand also eating, side by side. The folding dimension of the image causes these two horses to appear as if they are melded at the chest. Both heads eat, too, a splay of limbs. The photo has been affixed with a chalky layer and with curled ridges that meander through the upper right corner and the top center, pure black blob, as if the image of the horses is meant to cover up another something, darker, behind the first layer of the image, of the horses. In the bottom right corner of the image, a small white tendril spore of mold threatens to bloom. It is 4:37 p.m. right now which means my father is being served dinner in his new home. I have not been able to bring myself to go and see him but maybe three times since his transfer from the hospital, from our home. He walks with eyes averted downward. He has not shrunk in size as our mom has. The smell in this room where I am some days is of urine. Some days there is no smell. Behind the horses in the first layer of the image, in the background stands a building in the process of falling down. Its walls hold fast against a flat sky of blue so pale it almost matches with the grass; if the horses in the picture could learn to turn and walk up the image's two-dimensions, they could eat the sky, too, and make their bodies also from such food. In this image they will never lie down. Unlike my father's brain, the black blobs here will never grow. Of all the holes rendered in the building from its aging, through any of them all you can see are other parts of where despite itself the building continues day by day to stand.

WARDROBE

The image of the wardrobe bifurcates the frame into dark and light. It is a cold blue air, wherein the black traces of fainter black suggest a presence, something hid. For the first few minutes looking at the reflection presented in the mirror in the wardrobe I assume the room that contains this light is my parents' bedroom, where nights now my mother sleeps alone, still staying on her side of a bed she's shared for more than twenty years, resting four feet off the floor. A skylight over that bed has been muted, filled in with pink Styrofoam to keep the light on its own side. My father has not been back in this room for nine months up to today: long enough to birth another child. This room too would be the room set parallel to the same bathroom where nine months ago my father saw a man inside a mirror much like the one shaped in this image; a man, he said, who'd come to take him home. In trying to find a way to enter the mirror to go with this man, some version of him he no longer recognizes as himself, my father removed the mirror from the wall. The next day we took him to the hospital and he has not been back since. Looking longer at the image now I noticed, though, it is not my parents' room. The floor in the image is smooth and uncarpeted; the drapes bunch upon it as if hiding something tubular, made to droop. This room, then, is somewhere else; perhaps the guest bedroom in my sister's home, where no one that I know of ever sleeps. Or perhaps this image appeared on my sister's roll of film unasked, a phantom image, replaced inside her mind as someone she has been, the way most of what my father once took as daily grist is now surrendered to something else inside his head. This past weekend I went with Mom to see him for the first time in some time. He was sitting eating dinner in the dining area at a table by himself. He did not look up when we sat. He held the fork a certain way. He said he'd been at work. In the room at a table at the opposite end of that same room, diagonal from me, a woman with skin like the curtains in this image sang a refrain in a high and desperate tone, "They won't let us go home from here. There is no way to go home from here. They won't let us go. The water is too high." To the many others in the room the song went on without nod, as this was everyday, a new air accepted as wallpaper, as a little lock. Dad is on new medication timing, one which should make him less rowdy during night, as in recent weeks he's been getting angry as the sun leaves, trying to push other residents, trying to leave himself. Outside after dinner he is falling asleep every couple seconds. He gets up, refuses to sit. He points at the ground, at his black shoes with thick soles padded against the ground. "I can't believe that people who die come out with shoes like this," he says. "I'm gonna do it up good." He doesn't remember saying what he said the second after he says it. A woman watches us through the glass, her head obscured from outside by the sun above burning the surface into something half opaque. In this image of the wardrobe, it might be difficult to remember that the surface the mirror sits in can be opened, and does not lead outside, to the light. It is impossible to know by looking at the image what the wardrobe holds, even were we to stand before the wardrobe in this room today. Something about the light coming through the reflected mirror is terrifying: too bright. The only difference between a mirror and a window is a sheet of reflective paper. How many rooms are built primarily for sleep. There are no mirrors in the room my father lives in now except the one large one in the bathroom, doubling, as all mirrors do, the remainder of the room.

Untitled Photo

Moving backward from the center of the present moment as it exits my inside thinking of it, the progression of my father's dementing memory forms a film of familiarly linear burrows. There began in his days a smearing of the edges of rooms and ways and frames he'd used for years. Lost driving to the county where he grew up, in search of a house that since then has been dismantled. A bowl of cereal covered with saran wrap and put away inside the fridge. Sentences swerving off track in the color of his mouth as he stood in the kitchen where in other years he'd paid me cents on the tile to scrape away a bad layer of sealant, chipped away in crispy sleeves of white. Later, as his blue of days degraded, my father would begin to sense other homes outside our home. Pacing the house for hours waiting for someone to pick him up. Who. He often did not know their names, in his eyes the wheeling for the noun to climb on, a veil closing in the throat. Often when the people he could remember long enough to ask for by name did show, he did not recognize them, or had nothing made to say. Countless mornings waking in this house I would come from my own room along the hall past images of ourselves hung under glass to find new flowers on the table or the counter by the sink, a gift of no reason for my mother. Through his blood my father taught me how to dance. I did not let him show me how to shave my face, though I would now. Again in this image, as with the one of horses, there are the intruding colors: the chip of black along the top end; the white spore birthing out from the low side. Here the white has grown much larger than two frames before. It compliments the color of the bud. When my father was no longer allowed to drive his car, the curving doubled, as if bottled in the house, the pressing left him nowhere else to hide. Names left him. Mine did. Morgan's. Not always. A softening frustration in his eyes. Clinging to any recognition you would give him in the place where he no longer had himself. "It's like a golden rollercoaster," he said, on one of the last nights I can remember him looking me really in the eyes. "You got two wheel, six wheel, four wheel. You can get off the rollercoaster. I can be okay here." In this image, the flowers seem brand new. Since the time that they were taken, whenever that was, those flowers have changed color, crumpled, writhed. This image remains.

MY PARENT'S HOUSE

I t's been almost a year since I last sat down to look at the pictures. Since then my father has been moved home. He sleeps in a little bed at the foot of the bed where he used to sleep with my mother, where my mother now sleeps alone. The bed must be lined in plastic to make cleanup easier as Dad has become incontinent. The house is beginning in some small ways to smell like the way the group home did, though my mother cleans and cleans. Her patience is amazing, something I could hardly imagine in myself, and stronger than the walls. My sister has titled this picture *my parent's house*, making the possessive noun singular, a mistake perhaps, though not wholly incorrect. My father no longer has keys to the door here, and if he did he would not know how to use them. Through the afternoons he sits mostly at the kitchen table rubbing his hands or pounding the tabletop or drawing on papers in runic symbols and gibberish or nodding half asleep. He often does not look up when someone comes in or goes out. Any word spoken into him comes back malformed, spilled through little mazes behind his face, the corridors of those memory shuttles there slowly turning, growing fatter, bleeding into one another, toward one tone. The pale blue rectangle in the image butts up hard and fast against the edge of where the roof of the house ends in the photo's first square, a pale yellow lump massed in the bottom right hand corner seated like an immersed polyp, a canker on the flat. Its yellow is the same yellow of the house where under the lip of the roof we would come and go, heading out from this location of contained air that somehow continues to go on even when not watched; and the plane of the glass in the door that I once ran into at full speed, assuming in some now-forgotten terror that the door was open and would let me in and could. This is a house I've loved like any person, more so, this is a place where I do not have to change or age, that while my body does seem to be mumbling around me outside the hours here in here it is all mine. Where the wires go from the chimney we never burned a log in I have no idea; they seem to hold the house up. I wish that I could fold the two frames into one. I wish the layer of the blue sat over the house and made the sky unlike it is above the house, seeming deleted. I wish the polyp was on the eaves, another slick of junk that the day would wash away so easy instead of staying forever pressed into the unnamable mesh, though it is beautiful to see it there and not at all growing while in so many other places the unwanted thing does grow.

YELLOW DRESS

My sister is a woman. I think about her eyes moving in her head sometimes in rooms where she has gone to be herself with the man who lives with her and I can hear the muscles in her body around the lenses turn. The meat there that makes her is most like the meat of mine but how have the days changed our stations, curling out. My sister, the woman, is a woman, like my mother. I can feel them both sometimes beside me in any car, though when actually in a car with them I am mostly silent, and when I do speak it is terse. I don't know why. There are always dresses, even where there are not dresses. The yellow fabric drapes the shape of the air around my jowls, even though I have never thought about this dress before and likely will not again when this file and browser page is closed. So much to forget. A waiting season of gold again and gold again. There is a black beside the brightest and it is taking on the brightness, dissolving with it. It will not disappear but it will shift. I don't try to wonder if my father's memory condition is something that will come for me in the same way. It will or it won't. The white flecks in the dark of the picture aren't dust. I touch the screen of my computer where the image of the dark beside the dress is and the pixels in the LCD make it make pools, little whorls of no specific color. Beyond the dress the light makes somewhere else. There are so many yellows. They light the dress's spine. The straps of the dress seem to know more than the house does, but knowing what. They rest against the skin. Has my father ever seen my sister in this dress. Have I ever.

ALL MY BAGS ARE PACKED

This week my father wears all blue. He walks around the house from room to room not even looking. He goes where there is to go. The handle of the back door is pretend gold, a thin, primed finger. Spots of wear seem to age the skin of it where all of us have touched it for our own reasons, over and over, with or without something in our hands. Today Dad stands at the door and pulls and pulls the knob waiting for it to move again, though if it ever would he wouldn't likely step outside. There is nowhere to go out there, but it's an action without end inside this confine, and so a way to fill part of his day. My mother worries that the handle will soon break. "It's not going to open," I tell him calmly, pouring lukewarm coffee into a cup. "I know it," he says. He continues pulling. I really like this photo's frame. I like the way it eats into its image and reminds it to stay still as long as it can, for where it has moved is where the rotting color has come in. The red crust formed on the drapes or underneath them was not inside the house when it was photographed but now it is. The suitcase remains almost one-half covered over, or uncovered. The clasps don't seem to need a key. I can't think of what I would fill a suitcase with if I knew I was going to leave this house for the last time. Maybe just as much of the air as I could get to fit into it, something later to have to breathe.

BLOSSOMS

I shouldn't write any of this down. Any word I've ever written sticks to there and then there is a there there. It is the opposite of bloom. My thoughts are getting shorter, and me dumber. Do I believe that or is it something that I say. Days so fast they aren't days but liquids. The blooming clusters in this image couldn't hold on so much longer after they were printed in here, though in the image they are held. All I keep thinking of while looking at them is the pizza they would serve in my middle school lunchroom, the pepperonis cut in little cubes. I would eat the pizza into my body and be around other bodies whose names I can still hear said all aloud, though where they are now is someone else's picture. Am I really getting dumber. How much longer. The tuft of small white in the upper corner above the tree seems ready to spread down and wrap around it, come down from something large and alive beyond the frame. Or maybe the smoke came from the tree first and it is leaving. It doesn't matter. It is there. The dark of the limbs that raise the color up are thin and spindly and in this image need no base. The little packets of the flowers hold their laughter, and we must wait. ■

THE MAGIC MERGE

by Tracy Rose Keaton

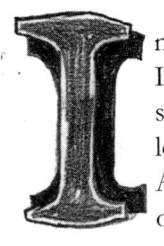n my tree house, that idealized, imaginary place I've built filled with all the things that give me space on this earth, I would like a shrine to the lowliest of goddesses: the groupie. She's an American invention, and she is the quintessence of feeling like nothing, an experience that never gets properly memorialized. Her submission is the kind that can only be found in the woman who is eternally a girl. Most women don't really want to think about the groupie anymore, but she is the place where most of us started. She is the ugly little hometown we all had to escape but never leaves us. She is the wide-eyed girl that wants to know what it's like to be with a boy, who believes that if we find the right one, it's all wrapped up, and that the world is golden. I spend a lot of time denigrating that part of myself, but she still chirps in my mind like a dime-store parakeet.

Where did she first raise her little disheveled head? It was the first time I sat on my daddy's lap and listened to his heartbeat. The first time I stared into his big brown eyes and wanted to live there. I had a silent one-ness with my dad when I was little that has only been equaled in my grown-up life once or twice. And when he left, whether it was for a day, or for good, those small experiences were the only ones I wanted. I think to be a true groupie there has to be a momentous separation from the father. His disappearance turns him into a magical, sparkly figure that must be pursued. This is what gives the groupie her edge.

As a young girl, I had a fantasy that David Bowie was my dad. My conscious mind really told the truth in this situation: not that he was my boyfriend, but that he was my dad. If he was my dad, he could never really leave, his magic and beauty would always be a part of me, part of my bloodstream. In that way, I was already a good little American consumer. Not only did I want him around physically, I wanted him to be a part of me cellularly. Why? Because I felt like nothing.

I've thought about all the groupies I've known: me, my mom, my best friend, maybe you, too. The groupie is the Harijan, "the untouchable" of the caste-system of American pop-culture. The one who plays clean-up for all the denizens of fame, who still keeps the hope alive that famous people (and perhaps men in general) are more than human. She is that poor little girl who will do anything—ditch biology, crawl through glass, give some head—to get a taste of the magic. All her actions point to the ol' standby that men (and famous people) are the only ones who've got the keys to the franchise of life.

The groupie is definitely a consumer who ends up getting eaten in the end. Not fabulous enough to be a concubine, or glamorously sinister enough to be a succubus, she is the everyday sort who puts on her rainbow-piped gym shorts and goes on a hunt for the magic penis.

I am describing her in too melancholic, harmless a fashion. Groupies, whether they are in the business of rock 'n' roll, law, or medicine can be some of the most revolting, scheming little bitches of all time. Their deep, yawning nothingness makes them that way. They can be as bad as any imperialist asshole when it comes to their need to conquer. No, friends, you won't be getting the *Almost Famous* version here. Where I come from, the groupie's got a bad overbite, some bleeding, super-skinned knees, and an aching, deranged heart.

Paul McCartney said that after the Beatles first U.S. tour, he thought Americans were the loneliest people in the world. Here we are, so young, the outcasts of the world. The poor self-esteem of the criminal and the religious fanatic is shot through our gene pool. We feel so bad, the only way to make up for it is to feel so, so, so good, and there is nothing like rock 'n' roll to rattle the mind's pleasure center like an atomic vibrator. It only makes sense that the American groupie is the most rabid, cannibalistic fan of them all. Surely, as we are nothing, the best way to catch that magic, make it a part of us, is to tear at, merge with, or optimally marry the source. The more evolved would say picking up the guitar would be a better option, but that takes too long. It is easier to eat it, suck it, or bathe in it.

Do you remember AM radio? Probably not. There was a time where it represented a beautiful, sonic Oz-like utopia to all the sad denizens of the Midwest, the place from which I hail. Gladys Knight and the Pips were followed by the Stones, who were followed by Terry Jacks; the high and low, the black and white, the mediocre and the sublime were all allowed to exist in one place. It was a quick and easy aural shot of transcendence.

The Scottish foursome The Bay City Rollers were the little neon-pink tulips that rose from AM radio's utopian soil, and every girl wanted more than a whiff.

The following is my encounter with these fragile boys, who were nearly devoured. Groupies of all sorts are not unlike the lotophagi of Greek mythology: island dwellers that got blindingly high by consuming the succulent lotus flower. Keep in mind that when this occurred, I was a child and did not yet feel like nothing.

"S-A-T-U-R-D-A-Y NIGHT!"

I was quite wee, and my very young daddy, who was an *illuminatus* of the local biz, was emceeing one of their shows. We went to our city's giant sports arena, where the Rollers were making a special appearance. My dad had one of those piss-like stadium beers in one hand and my sticky little hand in the other when we met the lads by their limousine.

The boys ascended from their black car, so pale and slender, their shoulders narrow, and their hair ornately chopped-up in beautiful plumage. They wore plaid pants in gleaming red and green, with their little hipbones jutting out. My first male love, my dad, was of hearty German-Norwegian stock with curly black hair and big broad shoulders. These men were like girls, bird-like and frail. They looked like me, except with weenies. Where was their daddy, I thought.

We followed the birdmen up these metal stairs to a scaffold. As the steel stairs squeaked underneath us, we were greeted by the most deafening roar of high ecstatic voices. It was the electric tone of a swarm of insects. I squinted into the lime green field, and all I could see was an ocean of plaid scarves waving, back and forth, back and forth.

I was standing next to the blonde member of the Rollers. He waved a tiny wave, a weak smile on his pale Scottish face. I was standing so close to him, I could feel the warmth coming off his body, but he wasn't there. It seemed to me, though I thought I must be crazy at the time, as if the insect sound was somehow sucking out his soul, and he was internally struggling against it, playing dead. I see now that this was probably true.

Later on we went to the show at another cavernous venue where they had livestock events and car shows. The show was sold out. My mom, sister, and I waited in the green room, where they had RC and Tab in a silver bucket. I ate a tiny Swiss cheese sandwich and sucked on an RC until it was time to go upstairs.

I felt it as soon as we started up the stairs, but "it" wasn't a part of me. It was a presence around us like smoke. I would later feel "it" inside my own body: that need to tear the wings off those little birdmen and rub their faces in my flat little chest. But I wasn't there yet. I didn't even think of myself as a girl.

The throng upstairs consisted of suburban girls, with round thighs in too-tight pants and awkwardly budding boobies in tiny t-shirts, screaming full-bodied, chest-heaving screams. Tears rolled down their faces, they seemed to be in physical pain, and yes, there was the sour smell of piss in the air. The place was dark and warm, and I felt instinctually that these girls were expressing something so utterly, utterly urgent.

The birdmen bobbed up and down, perpetually smiling. Suddenly girls were appearing on the stage, wrapping their bodies around the young men. Big dudes ran out of the wings, unwrapping the young girls from the birdmen's bodies and carrying them off the stage. There was one girl after another, and sometimes we would be only a couple feet away from them as they were dragged offstage.

I will never forget the girl who required four men to carry her off. She was spasming, her pink baby-tee pulled up around her chest to reveal soft white rolls of fat, her sad little face knit in anger and disappointment. "I JUST WANT TO TOUCH THEM! I JUST WANT TO TOUCH THEM!" she wailed over and over.

I remember my mom, who was probably only 13 years older than the girl, squeezing my shoulder and bringing me closer into her lambskin coat. I was absolutely stricken by the experience, didn't have the words for what I saw. If I could, I probably would have said: "Do you know how weird we are?"

* * *

By the time I was ten, I had watched enough television, looked at enough magazines, and weathered enough of my parents' misery to know that I was nothing. I knew it with fierce certainty, and slid further into a world of books and rock stars, and none of them had tits.

We return now to David Bowie, the first man to inspire any stirrings in my body. My dad lived in a dingbat bachelor pad with brown carpeting and dying ferns, and owned one of those highly coveted beta videotape machines. He taped a documentary about the history of rock 'n' roll hosted by the dreamy Jeff Bridges, who narrated the program wearing low slung jeans, walking on a L.A. beach. I watched this religiously every Wednesday that we slept there. The show featured a skinny, beautiful Bruce Springsteen doing "Rosalita" and the Eagles, replete with floppy hair and embroidered shirts.

The absolute climax of this program however, was to be found in David Bowie as Ziggy Stardust, who truly broke my groupie cherry. The moment of penetration occurred during a live performance of what I liked to call "Ziggy Played Guitar":

He is wearing a red samurai-style kimono cut just below his ass, exposing slender but strong ivory thighs. On his thin pale wrists hang big plastic lady's bracelets from the forties. He lunges, and then raises himself up into a pose with his legs wide apart and his long, pale arms outstretched. *I am your God*, the pose seems to say, *love me, worship me, eat me, do with me what thou wilt.*

The feeling I had watching this one moment was pure elation with a lust that was spiritual in nature. It came close to the feeling you get when you fly in your dreams. I would do anything, ditch biology, crawl through glass, give some head, for

I was literally trying to make the sound a part of me. It was almost as if by merging with my object of longing, I could be born again.

that feeling. My only option at the time was to play the moment over and over again in rapid succession, the proverbial addict taking hits off the pipe. Thank God it was on tape. My sister sat next to me on the brown velvet couch, absolutely helpless.

"Jeez," the nine-year-old said, "Do you know how weird you are?"

Yes, I had some idea.

My dad had Bowie's *Hunky Dory* LP, and I listened to it on headphones over and over in some dark corner, behind a rubber tree plant. I was literally trying to make the sound a part of me. It was almost as if by merging with my object of longing, I could be born again.

And so I trudged through life, half in a dream, thinking that one day the delightful merge I longed for—like the one on my dad's lap, like the one I had with the hi-fi would happen—and I would be complete. Over time, I would see the impossibility of the occurrence, but as I am an American, I knew there must be a way to overcome it.

* * *

One of my dad's longest-standing paramours was definitely a super-groupie. Tall and slender, with long raven hair, her ass was on the cover a 1972 "gentlemen's" mag, perched on a bicycle seat. Faye was my first experience of a real-live anima woman, the beautiful kind upon which men can project their most exalted, untouchable inner-femininity. My mom was pretty, but in that Midwestern, I-have-to-work-for-a-living way. Faye had the kind of beauty you only find in '70s foreign films: porcelain complexion, impossibly symmetrical and fragile in feature. Jerry Hall, Mick Jagger's longtime girlfriend, is Faye's spiritual sister, if not in reality, in her own private cosmology.

Faye lived in Athens in the early '70s with a bunch of American models who posed for *European Vogue*, and they were all in a race to nab famous husbands. There are tons of photos of them on white rocks by the sea, dressed Biba-girl style with scarves on their heads, embracing wrinkled old Greek fishermen.

"Your dad's really only a B-level celeb," she would say, "I believe I've failed."

We lived in rented apartments, and it was a big deal to go to a fondue restaurant on the weekends. She was a princess humoring the plebes. "Jesus Christ," she said, "my best friend ended up in a castle with one of the guys from Monty Python, for Christ's sake."

Faye had been with baseball players, even had a couple of dates with Shel Silverstein, and a short stint with the editor of a major arts magazine. She would spend her days in the slow, furtive nurture of her beauty, taking baths, eating cocktail onions out of the jar and smoking cigarettes. At night she gave the performances that would keep these powerful men around and her meals bought, as the carefree, fun-loving muse in the floppy hat. When they discovered who she really was, things got difficult.

Faye was, in fact, deadly intelligent, only making her task all the more impossible. She was a capable photographer and had a secret penchant for the lesbo-genius Virginia Woolf. Her mom was a showgirl nabbed by a rich Jewish textile tycoon, and in many ways Faye had been pruned into her destiny. I use the word "pruned," as I saw her consistently growing against her own better interests, according to her upbringing. In our long exchanges, where it seemed we were always the same age, Faye would have some shocking revelation about my dad or herself that would force her to shove many cigarettes in her mouth in awful succession.

"I don't think your dad really likes me very much," Faye said. "What do you think?"

"*D'accord*," I would answer back.

"Let's get the hell out of here," she would say, and we would abscond to some coffee shop where I would watch her smoke more cigarettes.

I knew instinctively that if Faye flourished too far, she risked that life-changing madness that would burn the truth right out of her, and so I kept my observations simple, and open to interpretation.

It became very apparent very early on that I was not going to follow in Faye's footsteps. I had been appraised of my physical flaws, some of which could only be changed with plastic surgeries that haven't yet been invented. "If only your eyes were wider apart," she said, "your nose smaller." Then I would have the magic. I could nab a rock star from the front row, just like she did. Then the world would be golden.

There is nothing worse than longing for a completely new physiognomy, and seeing no other recourse, I completely rebelled. Faye lived in a very simple world, where the primary motivating force of humanity was sensation and sexuality. My father seemed to agree, and acted the egregious sensate. Fuck them all, I thought. I am moving into the attic of my pale little body, and I'm never coming out, fuckers. This proved to be close to impossible.

* * *

As my dad was a demi-celebrity, the proverbial big Zeus in the small Olympus, and he was the quintessential dark-haired, denim-crotched babe in the '70s sense, there were women around constantly. And my dad had no problem availing himself of them, as if he lived in some 24-hour sex pharmacy. There was no lack of sexual healing in his life, but it was mixed with drugs, which gave it all the charm and gentility of che-motherapy. Nineteen-year-old auto show models, secretaries in frilly polyester shirts, football players' ex-wives with fake boobs, cigarette-voiced chick bartenders: there were loads of these seemingly blank yet anxious creatures waiting on that brown velvet couch. When they made it upstairs, their exchanges were brief, intense, and often very, very loud.

Faye had won, out of the pack of women who resembled Stepford Wives in their empty, vacated quality. I see now that they were all probably high. I hated them all. It was as if the Bay City Roller girls had grown bigger, meaner, and liked to use their fangs to eat drugs with their flowers. They gave less than

A question to all grown-ups: Do you know how weird you are?

a shit about me. And it was much easier to see my father as the victim, as the object of consumption, when, in the end, he was masterminding the bloodbath.

This to me was mating. This to me was heterosexuality. If my dad was any form of flora, he wasn't the pink-tulip kind. He was a big red mushroom that could get you very high. He was young, he was cute, he was famous and funny, and by all accounts, a good lay. He also had the good drugs. And he was miserable. What lost little girl between the ages of 18 and 45 could resist? A question to all grown-ups: Do you know how weird you are?

I realize now that I saw all women as groupies, or at least potential ones. There was no other paradigm that I was exposed to. I watched my single mom search for her indigent self almost predatorily, like so many divorced women of the time. Yoga and secretarial classes, wine-tasting parties and wilderness vacations were filled with the self-less refugees of bad marriages. I watched Faye consistently push her own reality down and away from herself in order to placate the magic mushroom. Sure, there was a feminist movement, but it had yet to liberate anyone I had known.

In the theater of life, I decided that I was not capable of being an anima woman, the only role offered me in my small reality, so I would become my own odd mixture of scowling misanthrope and cultural anthropologist in big black shoes. This would later become its own sort of female archetype, helped along by punk and new wave, and should also be duly represented in my tree house, but we'll get to that later. In keeping with the ol' cliché, rock 'n' roll (always and still does) came to my rescue. This is one of the most significant gifts (besides an inveterate childlike view of the world) my daddy gave to me.

One day my dad brought home the first Pretenders album and threw it on the brown velvet couch. He might as well have thrown a grenade.

On the cover, the band is standing in a Stanley Kubrick white void. The gorgeous alien in the middle, the brunette in red leather is a changeling: a little bit boy, and a little bit girl. The scowl on her face seems to say, "Hello, you callow fools, you have never ever heard anything like this before."

So there I was, bare feet in the brown shag, standing nervously at the record player, hiding myself behind the rubber tree plant. Like Charlie unwrapping the magic chocolate bar, I removed the black record from the white cover and gingerly placed it on the hi-fi, my pale little hands all a-tremble.

Hearing the first notes of the first song, "Precious," was like eating dark chocolate for the first time. The taste is weird at first, kinda bitter, but then suddenly it's all smooth and soft and you're inhaling it through your nose and eating more and more till it's all over your fingers and your mouth is all florid with dark sweetness. Her voice was syrup oozing over whizzy, wiry boy guitars that sounded like signals bouncing off UFOs.

And then from outta nowhere she sings, "FUCK OFF!"
Hey, wait a minute. What was THAT? Did I just HEAR that?
Let's play it again, let's see… okay… "Well-not-me-baby-I'm-too-precious-I-had-to-FUCK OFF!"
Oh my God. That's what she said. That's WHAT SHE SAID.

I played that little measure over and over again, till I was falling on the shag in gales of shocked adolescent laughter. I have no doubt that legions of repressed, knotted up little girls did the exact same thing, and our need to divide and conquer was born.

Of course, explaining the import of the Pretenders' arrival to a young girl now is like explaining how exotic and shocking Elvis was in the '50s. When I was growing up, girls simply did not play guitars. The only rock star with tits was the loveable Suzi Quatro as Leather Tuscadero from "Happy Days." Not to demean her in anyway, but to me, Leather didn't seem as formidable and drop-dead elegant as Miss Hynde. (Though there couldn't have been a Chrissie without a Leather, or for that matter, a Joan Jett. These ladies were the true shag-do pioneers.) I had never heard a lady sound so strong and threatening and calm. I was used to my white lady singers being sad like Joni Mitchell and Laura Nyro or desperate and on-the-edge like Janis Joplin. This lady was none of those things. She was goddamned rooted in her high-heel boots. Some of the oldies-but-goodies have Betty Friedan. I've got Chrissie Hynde.

I did further research and found out that the pop genius Ray Davies was her boyfriend. In pictures together they didn't look like Mick and Bianca, or even John and Yoko. They looked equal, almost twin-like. In my 11-year-old imaginings of their relationship, submission of any kind was completely impossible. There was no flower to be eaten, no souls to be lost in this union.

This is where I began to truly eat the flower, when I decided that I was going to take pop culture into myself, like the rest of the world with the Aniston shag-cut or the Pritikin diet. When I was 13, I took the album with me to my mom's hair-stylist and got my first trainer shag haircut. I was going to get to that brave new world if it killed me. If I had to rebuild cell by cell. And I almost did.

* * *

I plastered my room with pictures of rock stars and women throughout the ages with haunted, heavily made-up eyes: Theda Bara, Patti Smith, Siouxie, Clara Bow, Alice Cooper. In an act of transcendental groupiedom, I would sit hunch-shouldered on my Merimekko bedspread and meditate on these images for hours, hoping to drink in the pictures' essences and transform myself.

Every day in my mind was a salon at the Chelsea Hotel. Long-legged, black-haired boy poets (preferably pock-marked) lounged about like cats. Patti Smith was my best friend and would throw the I-Ching on my bedroom floor.

If I stayed just the way I was in my beige turtleneck and brown cords, no one would see the brave new world I had created. Not a one. My Chrissie haircut, however, was the first time my inner life asserted itself outward. And it was one of the best things I ever did. The shag really is a magical thing. It made David Bowie "Ziggy Stardust."

I became a sartorial samurai. There was no form of ripped

dress, fishnet or garter I would not wear. Some days I was a boy, and some days I was a girl. Sure I was lonely, but I was free. B.C. (before Chrissie) I was merely a phantom in the high school halls; A.C. I was a puzzling presence, and at best, someone to be FEARED.

My persona suggested a decadence and recklessness that was really a lie, until I encountered one of the most gorgeous mammals that had ever crossed my path. His name was Arthur, and my reaction to him was profoundly unsettling, to say the least.

I don't know when I started to discern this, but every time dear Arthur walked by, my heart and crotch would clench up, and the world looked like it was glowing in a Vaseline-smeared lens. My eyes could not leave the site of his silhouetted booty or the nape of his neck. He was the first real live boy I ever wanted to touch, he was my own Bay City Roller, and the sight of him made me grow big ol' FANGS. Some days you eat the flower, and some days the flower eats you.

* * *

There was a recklessness and a lack of fear of the world about Arthur that made me want to be near him as much as possible, bury my head in his flat chest, like the girls at the Rollers. But I had to do it without being noticed. I pretended a

Arthur had the great awkward bravado of the shat-upon geek. I could smell it on him… In reality, he was invisible just like me. At some point he knew he had to pull the great rock 'n' roll swindle and make a face.

casual repulsion for him, scowling at him over my notebooks, pretending he wasn't there, three feet away, when really I was trembling and sometimes nauseous. I studied his daily movements, and the smallest acts became fodder for slow, repetitive daydreams.

Arthur wore lip gloss and eyeliner to school, and dressed like a dime-store mod, in lime green suit jacket, impossibly tight pants, and white vans. He had a prominent nose like an English rock star, while everyone else at our school had their noses chopped into submission. I knew this was not an easy thing for a young man to carry, but he did, with head held arrogantly high.

He was always stirring up shit in the hallway, offending people with teenage blue humor (I heard him say the word "pussy") or playing Rick James too loud on his boom box. He carried himself in a slightly fey manner that freaked out the boys and made me want him more. For Halloween, he came to school dressed as John Delorean, a millionaire busted for coke, and pretended to snort powdered sugar out of a plastic bag.

Arthur had the great awkward bravado of the shat-upon geek. I could smell it on him. I did my research, and found a picture of him in an old yearbook. He was kind of pale, a bit amorphous in appearance. In reality, he was invisible just like me. At some point he knew he had to pull the great rock 'n' roll swindle and make a face. I knew he stared in the mirror just like me and said, "How do I make this work?" And he did. Arthur became a fixation, a constant jingle in my head. I thought maybe I could communicate with him telepathically and he would show up at my door and kiss me deeply. I realized the sensation, the need I was having was not unlike my need to merge with David Bowie. Speaking with him was out of the question, so I just memorized him, drank him in like a picture. I think that fixation was a form of visualization, because it all happened.

* * *

The whys and wherefores don't matter, but Arthur was my first real tongue-kiss.

He kept coming back to my little blue bedroom with the pictures of all my heroes falling off the walls, and we kept perfecting our make-out sessions, until I finally believed that I had mastered some small space of reality. His kisses were sweet and soft. Like me, he wore pancake on his zits, and every time we kissed he smelled like sweet make-up and clean adolescent sweat.

I thanked God every night for Arthur, and I thanked Chrissie, because suddenly I had my very own flower that I could inhale for as long and as deeply as I wanted. I knew it wouldn't have happened if I didn't have her aesthetic support. And I thanked her even more deeply when Arthur and I learned the art of the dry hump.

Yes, so that's what it was called. I had never seen it in the movies. Never heard it spoke of. As a grown up, it is a rare and lovely occurrence, and entirely underrated. I tried to talk to Arthur, and to listen to what he had to say. He was always funny, and sarcastic, but the whole time I just wanted to get on top of him and have at that lovely swelling hump under his jeans. Dear Arthur slowly and gently brought me out of the attic of my mind, and over time, we mastered a physical union as stirring and straightforward as a Ramones song. I like to call it the-three-chord-fuck.

I thought maybe that I had attained the cosmic co-mingling I longed for. Like the one where I lived in my dad's brown eyes. Like the one where I stewed in the magical strains of *Hunky Dory*. We made tapes for each other, documents of our inner universes. I floated in his and he floated in mine.

The complete lock-in occurred when Arthur brought a tape over that contained the pain and poetry of the Kinks. He said, "There's a song on here I think you'd like."

We lay down on the floor in my room in front of the boom box and listened to "Too Much on My Mind."

There's too much on my mind
There's too much in my mind
And I can't sleep at night thinkin'
About it
It's ruinin' my brain
I'll never be the same
My poor demented mind is slowly going
There's too much on my mind
And there's nothing I can do
About it

Yes, Arthur could see I was a nut. But he didn't run. He brought me songs to celebrate it. He was rejoicing in all the things that nobody saw. He saw me. And he wasn't going anywhere for a good long time. Thank you, Chrissie. Thank you, Ray.

* * *

Yes, friends, all flowers rot, if not tended to with delicacy and dedication. All great bands make awful records as time

Arthur and I were part of that grand experiment of the '70s, which was fueled by the spirit of rock 'n' roll... But you know Woodstock led to Altamont, and most of us kids were left dirty in the mud, lost in all the bad feedback.

goes by. There were many reasons why I was nuts. There were many reasons why Arthur possessed a desperate hum. When you are in the beginning throes of romance, those small, far-off alarms simply fade into your lovers' mix tapes. But just as bodies begin to droop, and hair grows in unwanted places, the love between Arthur and I became all too real and unpalatable. All the things that brought us together, as they say in the grand pop music tradition, drove us apart.

We both had unglamorous secrets, the squalid, warty kind they don't even talk about in foreign movies, or in sparkly Beatles songs, the secrets that the groupie and the shat-upon-geek-cum-rock-star are trying to run away from. I will not reveal them here, because it's really not the secret that counts. In this case, it's the effect. We were both abandoned in basic ways, not an uncommon occurrence for the children of the baby boomers, and eventually all the poison created by that primal loneliness just washed over the whole thing and killed it.

Arthur and I were part of that grand experiment of the '70s, which was fueled by the spirit of rock 'n' roll: "Fuck you, this is what I want, and I'm going to get it." It was only right. But you know Woodstock led to Altamont, and most of us kids were left dirty in the mud, lost in all the bad feedback. That was Arthur's desperate hum. That was the sharp noise in my head that made me nuts.

Actually, things went wrong when Arthur started playing in a band. It made me need him even more. He was my inner exalted male coming to life in front of me. Over the years Arthur and I broke up many times. He slept with other girls, and his innate charm turned into something aggressive and predatory. Somehow I always got him back. But suddenly the transaction that I had long feared was occurring. There was no more equality, no more bliss. The whole thing was taking on the tenor of sadism. He was my father, and I was one of those lost, empty bitches waiting on the brown velvet couch.

Submission in small tastes is delicious, but as a way of life, well, you'll end up with your head in the Easy-Bake oven. And in the end, as any S&M expert can tell you, submission is simply a sneaky form of control. Basically, I gave up everything that made my existence my own. I had an office job that paid for everything but left me exhausted and pissed off. I'd pay the rent so he could be an artist. I would take care of him as long as he would be my exalted inner male. Not that different than a guy with his trophy wife. ("Hey, baby, here's $1000—get some nice underwear.") I might as well have been hooked up to poor Arthur on an IV. I would tend to him like a flower, and he would go onstage to sing my song. He would be the one who would live in the eyes of others, and I would make sure he was presentable.

The role of muse is a fairly dangerous one, in my experience, fraught with insanity and blood loss. Yet it is so necessary to any creative transaction. As a muse, you're really just the plot device in someone else's drama. And, actually, sometimes the line between "muse" and "mother" is fairly negligible. I remember laying in bed late at night, our legs that had never seen the sun rubbing against each other, telling Arthur the breaks were too long between songs onstage ("Work some thing up, keep the momentum going!"). My spot-on insights poured out ("Wear the plaid pants, they look so good on you!"). I delivered these pronouncements with earnestness and urgency. Arthur eventually wrote a song called "Talking Doll," which I'm sure was an homage to my loquaciousness: "You're a talking doll, and you know it all, and you're not afraid to say it." But, honestly, I was just trying to help.

So there I was, looking up at Arthur and his guitar onstage, and he suddenly took on the hypnotic quality of a demi-god, at least to me. The traditional hierarchy was already in order. All the office-worker girlfriends were in the audience wearing their favorite nighttime rock 'n' roll finery—mini skirts, push-up bras, thigh high boots—stuff that got you noticed from the stage. We were all brimming with yearning, and if we were thirteen we would have been pissing ourselves. There wasn't one musician among us girls, not even a one who discussed their "creative interests." We were being sucked into the "good Midwestern girl" vortex, taking care of our *artistes*.

Don't do it. Because when he is gone, you will feel like your hands have been chopped off.

My only form of rebellion was to dress like a boy, which Arthur seemed to like anyway. I think all of us girls secretly hated each other. It was the kind of thing they talk about in feminist theory where women will destroy their competitors for the magic penis. I knew at least two of my friends wanted to get at Arthur's phantasmagorical weenie, and eventually they both did.

I'll never forget when Arthur told me one of his admirers was moving in with him. We were sitting in the house he shared with his band mates, the walls covered with forty-fives, the shelves littered with ashtrays and dirty bongs. He was wearing a "Jesus Loves Me" t-shirt and a scarf, a la Syd Barrett. I was wearing purple jeans and a Schlitz t-shirt, a la '90s androgynous dirt head. The girl, unlike me, had a sweet doll-like symmetrical face and a docile nature. All she wanted to do was help. There were organic vitamins by his bed that she bought for him, and strange hippie salves. She was a rock 'n' roll nurse.

When he uttered the words, "Rock 'n' roll nurse is moving her shit in this weekend," I hit him in the head with a couch cushion. Arthur was genuinely shocked, but there was no way he couldn't see it coming. After I hit him, I felt somehow satisfied. I cried and laughed right in his face, splattering his ironic t-shirt with tears and snot. "Jesus doesn't love you, oh no, he does not. And I don't either." Well, I actually did, and maybe Jesus did too. But if the rock 'n' roll nurse was moving in with him, it must really be the end.

It took me a very long time to get over Arthur. I went into shock, and he got married. Isn't that what men and women do?

* * *

So there I was with my hands chopped off, watching the ghost blood spurt out of the stumps. Ultimately, the yearning of the trod-upon groupie saved my life. The groupie goddess kept me listening to records, kept that little lovely flame in my sternum burning. The groupie is a good, loving sort at her core. She feels such immense pleasure, such a powerful sense of discovery, and all she wants to do is help. But like all good things in excess, the ecstasy of this young one can explode into self-immolation. It's important for the groupie to remember that it's not the singer, it's the song. The song you can listen to over and over, even learn to play on the piano. The singer might leave you with a pair of bloody stumps.

As is my dramatic nature, I believed that I could not love anyone but Arthur, that absolutely no one else could tolerate the sharp noise in my head, my deeply disturbing quirks. Arthur was the only one who could understand what it was like to feel so abandoned, but I couldn't talk to him about it because he was the one who was gone. He gave me more attention, in his own circuitousness way, more than anyone I had known.

I just couldn't see getting on top of anyone but Arthur, and anyone who wanted me to would have to hit me in the head with a couch cushion, or perhaps a brick, to make me see that I should. Eventually, that did happen, and when I finally fucked someone else I was so very shocked and sad that it wasn't Arthur. I am an odd sort, easily imprinted with other's fingerprints. I say this in hopes that you are just as odd.

So I decided that I would have to be my own inner exalted male. I thought that learning to play the guitar would be an anti-dote to abandonment sorrow. I would never be my mom or step-mom Faye, or any of those weird ladies on the couch. I would be rid of self-pity and self-doubt and all the things I felt had gotten me into trouble, and no one, no one could ever truly hurt me again, because the thing I loved most would be a part of me. I had to find out what the deal was with playing power chords, and I learned how to play them without any real affinity for the instrument, except for the knowledge that it was a thing of power, like a magic pirate sword, and I was going to hold it.

For so many years, playing music onstage had been this inscrutable, magical thing that I truly believed that if I played in a band I would hold the keys to the franchise of life. It would enable my need to fuck musicians to cease, my poked out eyes to grow back Elizabeth Taylor violet, my scars to peel off like silly putty, my chopped-off hands to be replaced with Pete Townshend's long, slender ones.

This is what I had projected on the musician for years: a sense of impossible elegance and wholeness. Even as I had read bios and researched the depths of their miserable lives, musician self-loathing seemed somehow mythical and so much more delicious than mine. Yeah, Brian Jones was a manic-depressive, but he looked so much better, all golden-haired and wrapped in Moroccan tapestry, being a paranoid asshole than I did. And he knew how to play the sitar. If I was in a band, all the things about me that I found repugnant would suddenly be beautiful, right?

I find it funny that I thought it would all be so simple. I think that's part of being an American, the hope that it will all be so simple. It's that adolescent consciousness that we have, that tragic vitality that ends up killing people: the magic bullet, the magic man, the magic pill. Eventually, I found myself onstage with a band at a local club, nervously, anemically strumming, staring out at a bunch of disaffected young people. Instead of being a girl out there, I was a girl up there, and I thought, "Is that all there is?"

The Guitar wasn't a magic sword. It was a big, slimy trout flopping around in my hands. Simply strumming in front of people without fainting at first was enough for me. Perhaps it was just that introductory self-hatred that flows so easily when you try something new, but my newly-grown hands seemed somehow aristocratic and soft. I couldn't even begin to think about the technical aspects of my Epiphone-Les-Paul-copy-with-the-broken pickups, I was so overwhelmed. And when such technicalities were discussed, I flatlined like I did when people talked about cars. How fucking stereotypically female of me, I would tell myself. You'd think I hadn't evolved at all.

It got easier, and I became a passable rhythm guitarist and a solid singer. But playing music involved lugging equipment. A LOT. No boys hit on me, EVER. No girls to speak of, either. And we had to fight just to keep the audience looking at us. I suppose if I was doing it for the music I could somehow be inviolate. But in reality, the meek little girl was doing it to feel somehow three dimensional, and I just wasn't rock 'n' roll nuts enough to throw myself around like Iggy or flash my tits like Courtney so that the monolithic father out there could see me.

I have always been aware that you can't take anything for granted, not even the ground beneath your feet, so I fought very hard for my little piece of the musical experience, and for the exact realization I DID NOT WANT. There was not going to be any magical merge with the universe, was there?

I couldn't avoid letting go of Arthur by being Arthur. I was never going to make the blind see. I know the kingdom of heaven is within, but I don't want to GO IN THERE.

It's so weird, that little groupie goddess, the one who got me in so much trouble in the first place, the one I was trying to ditch somewhere in some existential motel in the desert, is standing in front of that imaginary door going inward. She refuses to leave, because she just wants me to see her. That's all she really wants.

So for the first time I look into her eyes, and in a whimsical, avid way, they're saying: "Even if it's Amityville Horror in there, it's really just a movie, isn't it?" ■

RILEY & SONS, LLC
General Store & Mill
Stumps in front of store reserved for the old-timers!
So don't you dare sit on 'em. Or W.G. will give you a mouthful and then some.

CONTRIBUTORS

Blake Butler's most recent book is *Nothing* (Harper Perennial 2011). He lives in Atlanta.

Joshua Cohen is the author of the novels *Witz*, *A Heaven of Others*, and *Cadenza for the Schneidermann Violin Concerto*. In 2012 he published a collection of short fiction, *Four New Messages* (Graywolf Press). A nonfiction book, *A Short History of Attention*, will be published in 2013 (Notting Hill Editions).

Tracy Rose Keaton is a writer living in Los Angeles. Her work has appeared in periodicals, art, and gentleman's magazines, music websites, and on the stage. She's on a first name basis with most of the staff at the Astro Diner in Glendale, as well as the cranes who reside at the Silver Lake Reservoir. She is really happy to be included in *Frequencies* and to be working with Two Dollar Radio. She plans to publish her first novel this year.

Morgan Kendall is an Atlanta-based artist with a background in painting working primarily in photography. Her dreamlike images have been both published and exhibited internationally. You can view her portfolio online at flickr.com/photos/mkendall. She is online at morgankendallart.com.

Scott McClanahan is the writer of *Stories V!* and *The Collected Works of Scott McClanahan, Vol. 1*. Two Dollar Radio will release his book *Crapalachia* in 2013. New York Tyrant Books will release his book *Hill William* in 2013. He makes poem movies at hollerpresents.com.

About the Artist

John Gagliano is the house-artist for all issues of *Frequencies*, whose original artwork will grace each cover of the journal and whose illustrations will accompany every essay.

He was born in Floral Park, NY, and currently resides in Brooklyn. John completed some four years of art school at FIT and appreciates the fact that he doesn't limit himself to one medium or idea. However, acrylic seems to be his weapon of choice. In 2007 he joined Unruly Heir and fills a momentous role, creating unique prints, T-shirts, and brand illustrations that bestowed another dimension to his commercial work. His art has been shown throughout New York, and many other cities along the east coast.

johngagliano.com

FREQUENCIES

ARTFUL ESSAYS
Volume 2 ~ Spring 2013

COMING SPRING 2013

FREQUENCIES: VOLUME 2 WILL FEATURE:

ROXANE GAY on issues of belonging in Middle Class Black America, ALEX JUNG on the gay sex trade in Thailand, KATE ZAMBRENO on actress/director Barbara Loden, and more!

HOW TO GET INTO THE TWIN PALMS
A NOVEL BY KAROLINA WACLAWIAK
A Trade Paperback Original; 978-0-9832471-8-0; $16 US

"One of my favorite books this year."
—*The Rumpus*

"A vividly drawn portrait of Los Angeles inhabited by alienated immigrants, Russian gangsters, and sex-starved bingo-addicted octogenarians." —*Poets & Writers*

I'M TRYING TO REACH YOU
A NOVEL BY BARBARA BROWNING
A Trade Paperback Original; 978-0-9832471-1-1; $16 US

"A provocative novel... that blurs the boundaries between life and performance, dance, art, and viral video."
—*Slate Book Review*

"As entertaining as it is thought-provoking."
—*Publishers Weekly (Starred review)*

TERMITE PARADE
A NOVEL BY JOSHUA MOHR
A Trade Paperback Original; 978-0-9820151-6-2; $16 US
 ★ *Sacramento Bee* Best Read of 2010.

"[A] wry and unnerving story of bad love gone rotten. [Mohr] has a generous understanding of his characters, whom he describes with an intelligence and sensitivity that pulls you in. This is no small achievement." —*New York Times Book Review*

SOME THINGS THAT MEANT THE WORLD TO ME
A NOVEL BY JOSHUA MOHR
A Trade Paperback Original; 978-0-9820151-1-7; $15.50 US
 ★ *O, The Oprah Magazine* '10 Terrific Reads of 2009.'

"Charles Bukowski fans will dig the grit in this seedy novel, a poetic rendering of postmodern San Francisco."
—*O, The Oprah Magazine*

RADIO IRIS
A NOVEL BY ANNE-MARIE KINNEY
A Trade Paperback Original; 978-0-9832471-7-3; $16 US

"Kinney is a Southern California Camus."
—*Los Angeles Magazine*

"A noirish nod to the monotony of work."
—*O: The Oprah Magazone*

BABY GEISHA
STORIES BY TRINIE DALTON
A Trade Paperback Original; 978-0-9832471-0-4; $16 US

"[The stories] feel like brilliant sexual fairy tales on drugs. Dalton writes of self-discovery and sex with a knowing humility and humor." —*Interview Magazine*

DAMASCUS
A NOVEL BY JOSHUA MOHR
A Trade Paperback Original; 978-0-9826848-9-4; $16.00 US

"*Damascus* succeeds in conveying a big-hearted vision."
—*The Wall Street Journal*

"Nails the atmosphere of a San Francisco still breathing in the smoke that lingers from the days of Jim Jones and Dan White." —*New York Times Book Review*

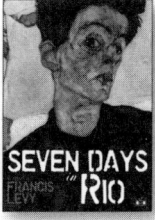

SEVEN DAYS IN RIO
A NOVEL BY FRANCIS LEVY
A Trade Paperback Original; 978-0-9826848-7-0; $16.00 US

"The funniest American novel since Sam Lipsyte's *The Ask*."
—*Village Voice*

"Like an erotic version of Luis Bunuel's *The Discreet Charm of the Bourgeoisie*." —*The Cult*

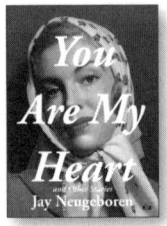

YOU ARE MY HEART AND OTHER STORIES
STORIES BY JAY NEUGEBOREN
A Trade Paperback Original; 978-0-9826848-8-7; $16 US

"[Neugeboren] might not be as famous as some of his compeers, like Philip Roth or John Updike, but it's becoming increasingly harder to argue that he's any less talented… dazzlingly smart and deeply felt."
—Michael Schaub, *Kirkus Reviews*

THE ORANGE EATS CREEPS
A NOVEL BY GRACE KRILANOVICH
A Trade Paperback Original; 978-0-9820151-8-6; $16 US
* National Book Foundation 2010 '5 Under 35' Selection.
* *NPR* Best Books of 2010.
* *The Believer* Book Award Finalist.

"Krilanovich's work will make you believe that new ways of storytelling are still emerging from the margins." —*NPR*

THE VISITING SUIT
A NOVEL BY XIAODA XIAO
A Trade Paperback Original; 978-0-9820151-7-9; $16.50 US
"[Xiao] recount[s] his struggle in sometimes unexpectedly lovely detail. Against great odds, in the grimmest of settings, he manages to find good in the darkness."
—Lori Soderlind, *New York Times Book Review*

THE PEOPLE WHO WATCHED HER PASS BY
A NOVEL BY SCOTT BRADFIELD
A Trade Paperback Original; 978-0-9820151-5-5; $14.50 US

"Challenging [and] original… A billowy adventure of a book. In a book that supplies few answers, Bradfield's lavish eloquence is the presiding constant."
—*New York Times Book Review*

THE DROP EDGE OF YONDER
A NOVEL BY RUDOLPH WURLITZER
A Trade Paperback Original; 978-0-9763895-5-2; $15.00 US
* *Time Out New York*'s Best Book of 2008.
* *ForeWord* Magazine 2008 Gold Medal in Literary Fiction.
"A picaresque American *Book of the Dead*... in the tradition
of Thomas Pynchon, Joseph Heller, Kurt Vonnegut, and
Terry Southern." —*Los Angeles Times*

NOG
A NOVEL BY RUDOLPH WURLITZER
A Trade Paperback Original; 978-0-9820151-2-4; $15.50 US

"[*Nog*'s] combo of Samuel Beckett syntax and hippie-era
freakiness mapped out new literary territory for generations
to come."
—*Time Out New York*

FLATS / QUAKE
TWO CLASSIC NOVELS BY RUDOLPH WURLITZER
Trade Paperback; 978-0-9820151-4-8; $17 US

"Together they provide a tour of the dissolution of identity
that was daily life in the sixties."
—Michael Silverblatt, *KCRW's Bookworm*

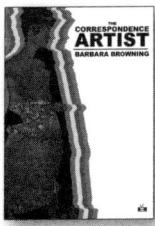

THE CORRESPONDENCE ARTIST
A NOVEL BY BARBARA BROWNING
A Trade Paperback Original; 978-0-9820151-9-3; $16 US

"A deft look at modern life that's both witty and devastating."
—*Nylon*